Speech! Speech!

Books by Geoffrey Hill

POETRY

For the Unfallen

King Log

Mercian Hymns

Tenebræ

The Mystery of the Charity of Charles Péguy

New and Collected Poems, 1952–1992

Canaan

The Triumph of Love

Speech! Speech!

PROSE

The Lords of Limit:
Essays on Literature and Ideas

The Enemy's Country:
Words, Contexture, and Other Circumstances of Language

POETIC DRAMA

Henrik Ibsen's 'Brand':
A Version for the Stage

Speech! Speech!

Geoffrey Hill

COUNTERPOINT
Washington, D.C.

Library of Congress Cataloging-in-Publication Data

Hill, Geoffrey
Speech! Speech!/Geoffrey Hill.
p. cm.
ISBN 1-58243-098-5 (alk. paper)
I. Title.
PR6015.I4735 S66 2000
821'.914 — dc21   00-055493

Book design and composition by Wesley B. Tanner/Passim Editions
Set in Monotype Spectrum

Printed in the United States of America on acid-free paper that meets the
American National Standards Institute Z39—48 Standard ∞

COUNTERPOINT
P.O. Box 65793
Washington, D.C. 20035-5793

Counterpoint is a member of the Perseus Books Group.

FIRST EDITION

In memory of David Wright

AT TUBA TERRIBILI
SONITU TARATANTARA
DIXIT.

Ennius

VORHANG,
BEVOR DU DEN BEIFALL
BEGREIFST.

Günter Grass

Speech! Speech!

1

Erudition. Pain. Light. Imagine it great
unavoidable work; although: heroic
verse a non-starter, says PEOPLE. Some believe
we over-employ our gifts. Given identical
street parties, confusion, rapid exposure,
practise self-emulation: music for crossed
hands; for two fingers; music
for taxiing to take-off; for cremation.
Archaic means | files pillaged and erased
in one generation. Judge the distance.
Innocent bystanders on stand-by. Painful
scenes mar final auto-da-fé.

2

Interpose a fire-curtain; stop the applause
from getting through. But would Herr Grass accept
the dedication — our names
unromantically linked? I owe him; he
owes me nothing. Here's an awkward
question | going spáre to be asked: dó
you, as Í do, sit late by the Aga
with clues received from sputtering
agents of Marconi; from Imre Nagy;
from Scott of the Antarctic frozen in time
before the first crossword? Decent old Böll —
why me, why not Günter? Help him, someone.

3

How is it tuned, how can it be un-
tuned, with lithium, this harp of nerves? Fare well
my daimon, inconstant
measures, mood- and mind-stress, heart's rhythm
suspensive; earth-stalled the wings of suspension.
To persist without sureties take
any accommodation. What if Scattergood
Commodity took all? Very well you
shall have on demand, by return, *presto*,
my contractual retraction.
Laser it off the barcode or simply
cut here —

4

Reformation woodcuts enscrolled such things
between the lips of magistrates, prophets,
and visionary infants. To me it sounds
like communications breakdown, somebody
promoting his (say her) fanatical
expressionless self-creation on a stuck track.
Our show-host has died many times; the words
of welcome dismiss us.
Anomie is as good a word as any;
so pick any; who on earth will protest?
Whatever is said now I shall believe it
of the unnamed god.

5

Enforcer! What will you have? What can I
freely give you? The usual twist
perfected with some pain. Remind me:
for how long did my guardian spirit
cry out under your interrogation?
What intact part of her was found
to sate your inquiry? *Salaam. Shalom.*
Napoo Finee. Finally, dental records.
Strengthen your signal I AM LOSING YOU. That
always gets to them. Reglue the fetish
pig made of terra cotta. Remind me:
bienvenue — is that arrival or welcome?

6

They invested — were invested — in proprieties,
where cost can outweigh reward. Decency, duty,
fell through the floorboards (*applause*). I cannot
do more now than gape or grin
haplessly. On self-advisement I erased
WE, though I [|] is a shade too painful, even
among these figures tying confession
to parody (*laughter*). But surely that's
not all? Rorke's Drift, the great-furnaced
ships off Jutland? They have their own
grandeur, those formal impromptus played
on instruments of the period (*speech! speech!*).

7

Not all they coúld do they háve done; but bring
atonement beyond dispute. Harps
in Beulah. In Hut Eight the rotors. So few
among many true arbiters: thát much
is already knowledge. Now to admit
heroes of lost chance, profundity's
astronauts missing their stars; their breakages
chargeable to all parties. Still, broken
ingemination, they cannot
charge us again for that. Claimant
Fatality appears and acts
mannerist through and through. Citations please.

8

Be stiffened by rectitude [|] kept
rigid with indecision. Say: coherence
though not at any price. Would I exchange
my best gift, say, for new spools of applause,
roulette set pieces (YOU OWE US MONEY)?
Cameo actors can make killings
their legacies. Even so [|] dereliction
is seminal, to the zillionth power
indicted (*vide* Augustine). But for that
primal occasion I cannot believe us
absolutely struck off. And – yes – Lilith
we háve met [|] and do I knów you?

9

Going ¦ attrition. Give me any advance
on attrition. Eternal progress? To the unseen
man in the corner, now gone. I will not
put up anyhow ¦ to attract their tictac.
This being the centennial of some half-
heard plea I AM AND HAVE NOTHING pass
round the one remnant candle of vigilance.
Most things are still in the dark. Í should be,
not glad, but able, to recall these wíth you
at sóme time, rabbi, sometime this century,
as they are here — immediate — to our powers.
But *welch ein Gruss*, what kind of pitch is that?

10

From the beginning the question how to end
has been part of the act. One cannot have sex
fantasies (any way) as the final
answer to life. Shiftless,
we are working at it, butt-headed
Sothsegger for one, between bouts of sleep
and community arm-wrestling, elbows
in spilt beer. TALK ABOUT LAUGH, TALK ABOUT
ANGRY. But don't count, don't bet,
on who or what ends uppermost, the franchise
of slavishness being free to all comers
without distinction.

11

Is MUST a true imperative of OUGHT? Is it
that which impels? In the small hours a red
biro clown-paints my pyjamas. Mirrors
disclose no exit-wound. Scrupulosity
unnerved so | *gelassenheit* is a becoming
right order, heart's ease, a gift in faith,
most difficult among freedoms. That's
fair enough, given injustice. Each strafe
throws in some duds, freak chances. The libido
of eunuchs, they say, is terrible. God
how I'd like to, if I could only,
shuffle off alive.

12

I have the instructions. Nów they read REMIT
NOTHING AT THÍS TIME BUT REFER YOUR PAIN —
you being me. Excuse us, please. The rules:
they stand for our redemption. Or whatever.
Your heart has to be in it, swiftly
and sharply dealt with, but alive
to its own beating; sometimes likened,
by misconception, to a creative
phase of the moment. How is it you were clad —
Balzac, you said — in the wild ass's skin?
Penitence easy-over. Penance | blood
from the leper's dish.

13

If I am failing you sense this ⏐ a blind
date of exclusion; the milieux, each mêlée,
whether in wrath, or hope, or enraged sorrow.
This for Max Perutz, brilliant alien star
of observation. Always our blind Fates.
Inheritance is a power among powers
out of its keeping. To these ⏐
honours, titles, are like wreaths delivered
in the name of the PEOPLE; that is to say
in name only. The acclaimed chorus
overrehearses silence. Listen: I ám – this
also ís – broken. For instance see *passim*.

14

What is it you seek and are caught seeking
in mirrors, for variety? The grammarians'
so-called accusative of recollection: thát ís,
recollection in the act? VARIETY
seems a misnomer if ⏐ when it sustains
Abraham weeping for Sarah ánd Hagar's
travail. Having through-revised the instruction,
make mourning instrumental. Spare us
a little ⏐ for what follows: axiomatic
redemption grafted to the condemned stock
of original justice; contestant juries
dealing out faith for faith.

15

About time and about this time [|] when all
her days are fulfilled: as at Pentecost
or at the Nativity, the Godhead
wíth her in spirit, like a flint arrow-
head touched to a vapour, a flame. *Intacta,*
through many roads despoiled. The bride of tongues
intimately perfect, perfect though untimely;
not our day. Believe it [|] Augustine
saved himself for this: the City of God
riding her storm-sewers, towering
at watch and ward, prophetic, exposed
to obscurity, hidden in revelation.

16

First day of the first week: rain
on perennial ground cover, a sheen
like oil of verdure where the rock shows through;
dark ochre patched more dark, with stubborn glaze;
rough soggy drystone clinging to the fell,
broken by hawthorns. What survives
of memory [|] you can call indigenous
if you recall anything. Finally
untranscribable, that which ís [|] wrests back
more than can be revived; inuring us
through deprivation [|] below and beyond life,
hard-come-by loss of self [|] self's restitution.

17

That's nót WORKERS' PLAYTIME. Trust Dad
to find the wrong wavelength. Trust Aunty Beeb
to screech like a tart. Trust the Old Man
to pawn his dentures. Trust Grandma to have to go.
Trust Ted-next-door to swear that his stuffed
parrot still talks. Trust Irish Jim
to call it a grand wake. Trust rich Uncle Tony
to drink from the saucer because we're watching,
and because he's rich. Trust Mad Bess
to queen it in purple. Trust your Mother
to notice who's missing. Trust Sandy
MacPherson to blow us to Kingdom Come.

18

Who nów says the divine spirit does grammar
to the power *x*? I want. You want.
You want I should write. Write whát ⏐ I ask.
Like, write this down, maybe. BEHOLDEN ⏐
I love it. Tell me ⏐ when were we ever
nót beholden? And yes, righteousness
sticks át it íf unrecognized. Steadfast
witnesses you might have called us ⏐ pharisees
not philistines. Rate zero on RECENT PAST
AS DISTRESSED SUBTEXT. Penalties. Plead
fax or e-mail. Cut out the funny speech.
Commit to landfill. Or recycle waste.

19

For stately archaic detail | tag Dürer's
LORD MORLEY with POMEGRANATE: self-shielding,
facet-compacted, its glitter-heart scarce-
broken | FIDUCIA. Go easy: think GRENADE.
Faithfulness wrong-footed (this, now, in re
Colonel F. Fajuyi, late Nigerian Army)
asks and receives praise-songs in lieu. The sun
scans Cancer to Capricorn: emergent
cohorts | mass for mutation. Semiotics
rule | semiautomatics: is the surreal
any more our defence? Call the tribunals
to order | but not right now.

20

THEY tell you that? Spiritual osmosis
mystique of argot — I like the gestures
that come wíth it: a kind of dumb thieves' cant.
SPI—RI—TU—ALI—TY | I salute you.
Ich kann nicht anders. It was not so much
cultic pathology I had in mind
as ethical satire; but you wriggle so,
old shape-shifter. Since I am compromised
I shall say more. Assume the earphones. Not
music. Hebrew. Poetry aspires
to the condition of Hebrew. Say that it ís
a wind in the mulberry trees: who will know?

SURREAL is natural | só you can discount
ethics and suchlike. Try perpetuity
in vitro, find out how far is HOW FAR.
I'd call that self | inflicted. Pitch it
to the CHORUS like admonition. Stoics
have answers, but nót one I go for.
Think surreal | the loss of peripheral
vision vis-à-vis conduct. See if Í care
any less than did Desnos, but he cannot
now be recovered | sight unseen. Body
language my eye. Regarding the shrimp
as predator: EYE TO EYE IT IS TRUE.

Age of mass consent: go global with her.
Challenge satellite failure, the primal
violent day-star moody as Herod.
Forget nothing. Reprieve no-one. Exempt
only her bloodline's *jus natalium*.
Pledge to immoderacy the outraged
hardly forgiven mourning of the PEOPLE,
inexorable, though in compliance,
media-conjured. Inscrutable Í call
her spirit nów on this island: memory
subsiding into darkness | nowhere
coming to rest.

It has its own voice, certainly, though that
fails to come through. Try Hilversum. The Dutch
are heroes | living as they have to. Give
Luxembourg a miss for old times' sake.
Recall the atmospherics. Stoicism
may well serve | fill its own vacancy.
Step forward, you. Speak at the red light.
What else proclaims us? More suggestions please.
Autographed hate-mail preferred. Everything sounds
THE CRY OF THE AFFLICTED. Thát any cause
to delete other options? Talk me thróugh this,
Gallant Little Belgium | I still hear you.

Diminishment | the long-withheld secret
of dying. The mind's threatened attention spared
by what it gives up; as by these dark
roses in rain-bleached tubs. Things to be taken
further | let me confess. Strategies
are not salvation: fár fróm it. Even so
REDUCE means LEAD BACK (into the right way),
mortal self-recognition. Patience
is hard, reductive. What comes next?
What shall I say: we múst be animal
to some purpose? My God, who else heard UN-
HINGE YOUR JAW, DO IT LIKE A PYTHON | and díd she?

25

As I believe I heard ┊ the astounding
percussionist is deaf. David said once
he could draw music up through heel of hand
(not Saul's David; David of DEAFNESS, late,
silenced by throat cancer) though the instrument
in this connection was indeed a harp.
Sympathy is more material than empathy:
só I interpret your response as you
register such *unbeschreiblich* . . . Luck
is against the many; and to be gifted
as she is álso with striking
and instrumental beauty ┊ cannot be bad.

26

No time at all really ┊ a thousand years.
When are computers peerless, folk
festivals not health hazards? Why and how
in these orations do I twist my text?
APPLY FOR FAST RELIEF. Dystopia
on Internet: profiles of the new age;
great gifts unprized; craven audacity's
shockers; glow-in-the-dark geriatric
wigs from old candy-floss (*cat-calls, cheers*).
Starved fourteenth-century mystics write of LOVE.
When in doubt perform. Stick to the much-used
CHECKMATE condom (*laughter, cries of 'shame'*).

Something of London shook itself apart —
vibrant Yiddish Theatre — was swept away
with the street-flares of Whitechapel. It was not
music to all ears. Rosenberg mostly
ignored it | as he avoided Hebrew. His LOUSE
HUNTING, nonetheless, remakes, re-masters,
redeems farce. He did not wholly imagine
rats, lice, the sole victors. His last efforts
to survive — like THROUGH THESE PALE COLD DAYS —
appear belated and timely acts
of atonement. Are you serious? Well I'm |
not joking exactly.

LONG TERM counted as thirty days. Hoarding,
looting, twinned by nature. Haruspicate
over the unmentionable, the occult signs
of bladder and bowel. More mental | hygiene
urgently called for | to forget oneself.
THOSE WHOM IN IGNORANCE I HAVE KNOWN
AND CHARMED BARREN. Scrupulosity can kill
like inattention. How will this be judged?
How shall I plead as one greatly
gifted with hindsight: those dead and dying
dropped there to maim the irresistible
beauty of the advance?

The sanctuary hung with entrails. Blood
on the sackcloth. And still we are not
word-perfect. HARUSPICATE; what does thát
say to you? CLEARING YOUR THROAT. Between us
is the Pope to be trusted? Cán he divide
night from day? What is his sphere of desire?
What price the menorah's one-octave
chant of candles? No-hope to redeem
all covenants. In visions you can tell
NOTHING has changed. Now as ever the sun
roárs, is black-rimmed, the moon burns, fire
quenches water.

Symbolic labour spinning straw to gold.
Not the hard labour of procrastination.
However you look at it you might
fancy yourself saved by some careless genie
numerate but illiterate. Courtesy
titles re-auctioned like licence plates.
Rage here as variant hobby. Proclaim
NO SWEAT in the tongues — coarse triumphalist
Australian-Tuscan. Culture shock — in fact
there's nothing to it. I mean | make real
your fantasy. What did I tell you — see —
they can't touch us.

31

This WORD | the word you are so strenuously
enacting: could it be CHARADE? Or CHIE?
Nót CHIE? *Merde* then | I pass. Daumier
was his latest Muse: now there's a thought
difficult to let drop. Even at the end
I overreach your stake with the viziers.
Soccer versus Islam. Ríp through thís lot:
END OF THE WORLD CUP. GO EASY WI' T' SENNA.
PECCAVI RESCINDED. THE AMUSEMENT
PARK TWISTER AND OTHER STORIES. MORE FAUNA
OF THE AUGEAN. BELT UP. PHAZZ. TAKE
TIME OUT, SIMONE WEIL.

32

Take issue. About time. Why not shout down
darkness above all? Invent the telegraph
you would be wise to. Some go
dancing, some set fire to their beds.
Anyone for a mock-up? It is not
easy to make do or make
reparation. MAKE ANSWER here
submits a bulk recognizance: e.g.,
as to the brain a telling of lost sensation;
as in heart's blood | slammers against appeal;
if instress | then with unselfknowing temper
confessional to the bone.

33

YES, I know: fantasies see us out
like a general amnesty, with *son*
et lumière and civic freedoms.
Something múst give, make common cause,
in frank exchange with defamation.
So talk telegraphese, say: FORTITUDE
NEVER MY FORTE. BLOOD-IN-URINE SAMPLES
RUIN EURO-CULTURE. Try NO to eách
succession of expenses; nominal
acceptance, each makeshift honour botched
as though by royal appointment. And PASS to all
duties, rights, privileges, of despair.

34

That caught-short trot-pace of early film: did minds
adjust automatically then? Coúld they
watch the stiff gallantry jig-jog, go knees up
into, half-over, the wire ⎟ follow it and know
this was nót farce – whatever else in thát line
might get them howling, have them dress ranks
to Chaplin's forwards-backwards fame and luck?
Such formalities! Thís after a rare
projection of WINGS: heroic lip-readers
in action – one last sortie and – bingo! –
ventriloquists on sight, choked mouthings PER
ARDUA, the eloquent belly-blood.

35

Say you dispute the audit – no offence
to her intended (or to her intended) –
pending the hierarchies so soon to be
remade ˈ though not with her demotic splendour.
Fantastic, apocryphal, near fatalistic
love of one's country ˈ bearing with it
always something under- or over-subscribed,
bound to its modicum of the outrageous,
cartoon-animation: jovial, martial,
charwomen, their armour bristles and pails,
dancing – marching – in and out of time –
to Holst's JUPITER ˈ ás to JERUSALEM.

36

Huntress? No not thát huntress but some
other creature of fable. And then for her ˈ
like being hunted. Or inescapably
beholden (this should sound tired but not
emotional to excess). Half forgotten
in one lifetime the funeral sentences
instantly resurrected – hów can they do it?
Whatever of our loves here lies apart:
whatever it is ˈ you look for in sleep:
simple bio-degradation, a slather
of half-rotted black willow leaves
at the lake's edge.

37

These I imagine are the humble homes
the egalitarian anti-élitist SUN
condescends to daily. Democracy
is in the voice — Churchill's or some other —
I cannot now hear; and the missing clue
WANHOPE: missing, that is, from the game
celebrity plays us for; not lost, since I
still seem to possess it. You too, Jack! —
know who I mean, eh? — poet and scholar
caught sashaying your shadow self. Say that
at normal walking speed, toes on the line.
Say: SURE SUCCESS OF RAP PAR FOR THE COURSE.

38

Do nothing but assume the PEOPLE'S voice,
its speaking looks of dumb insolence.
Xenophobic still │ the Brits are heroes
living as they have to — short-cuts, thwartings,
one circus act after another, the Powers
enlightened, vengeful: no darkness more
difficult of encounter. Show the folks
Caravaggio's FLAGELLATION — what's it worth? —
sensational, unfeeling. Award
damages for and against the press.
Why is the wreck still singing? All at once
to speak well of thís — A FINE STORY!

39

All right push off [|] any second and Í
have outlived you. Your pioneer flight
not mistimed, albeit without coverage.
How aboút thát: light-heavy solid husk
the body in perspective striking
absently – almost – on ribs of coal-staithes,
and blistered hardtop. How *nerdlich* to probe
sick personality – each stagnant
puddle a maelstrom? Describe being
in shock [|] Í'll sáy. ÓR what routine
visionary surveillance has failed
to return from patrol.

40

The Poles are heroes living as they have to
(put PAYABLE TO BEARER): the exploded
city they made fly [|] together again,
courtesy of Canaletto and the PEOPLE.
Gouvernement Géneral a drawn furnace
of things unmentionable. So thát
would be your lot then would it or is there more
Germanic-Slavic mirth? Like *Galgenfreude*,
hideous place-names long ago tattooed
into our bones. Brush-up mnemonics. Unearth
survival kit. Activate motto (the Poles
et cetera). Change date of expiry.

41

And what would not be Lusitanian
sorrow ⏐ were you to raise it: is this
rhetoric? Write NO or NO COMMENT. Hands up
all those too easily won over — *hoch*
to *Hochzeit*. Dreadful translations. Give out
the IOUs. The Christmas of the truce
even as it was ⏐ was passing: fróm and fór them.
Take that man's name and voice, Sarn't, íf you
júdge him unfít to match late-night *dévots*,
spoilsports from Devil's Island, Fenian Men
bloody and sententious, the Stahlhelm
trumpeted, the Lambeg pounding its beat.

42

Grace to withdraw — enter — an appeal ⏐ íf
there is leeway? Recídivist Í ⏐ shall
restore a lost glory to your circuits.
So argue righteousness, fee'd by the drab
ill-fortune of the Rand. Confess, Sir
Edward (alias Marshall) Hall,
I merit my nark's wages. As, at times,
you played to be unmasked. Here we are: caught
with eau-de-Luce, vitriol, defiling *Pearl*.
No, no; not a word. The jury is oút, húng
on forensic oratory. Your last defence
laughed us to tears.

43

You must be blind | VERITAS to stare so.
In the required half-minute it sounds good
to cast our intercessions | for the grand
chefs of World Order. Still: how to attest
with least defilement? Sieve it? Not that.
Authorize the inauthentic with sincere
fraudulence of empathy. Is there some
precedent for my 'slanders': in the Roman
love elegists, or perhaps three-headed
PUBLIUS, who cannot now be released
from the FEDERALIST PAPERS, a monster
of exact foresight?

44

It now seems probable that I have had
a vision or seizure — some stroke of luck
(see thirty-nine, *supra*). HE'S GOT A NERVE!
Cross-hatch the basilisk behind bars.
Cryptic third-degree: is the dandelion
alone parthenogenic, strange virgin tribe
of scorched earth? STOP WRITING. HANDS ON HEADS.
Meanwhile, without our knowledge, the conjectured
difficult child begins to understand
history. Do not refuse him his loss:
wanting things to change and to stay; briefly
comforted by snowfall.

Shocks, alignments, brake-fluids, slackened
memory, checked and adjusted. No, not
MORTIFIED. That was last season's key.
How strange it sounds, a fable of common
life: like Thánksgiving — neither
at one with the wórld nór with ourselves. GO HOME |
ŒCONOMY. A word pertaining to households,
inoperative, at the heart. And you,
a shade importunate. Least said; this said;
to be said at least: Íf I can see my own
way to forgiveness | I am MERCY your
blind | daughter.

Champ d'honneur versus *Schlachtfeld*: from this
affray | Prussia emerges the clear victor.
Is VECTOR now more widely used — if so,
hów exactly? *Die Zuckerzange, bitte!*
Please pass the forceps — you míght have said.
Tea with the Hohenzollerns. All the best.
Had fállen by thís time | my own ticket
long overdue. Somewhere in No Man's Land
I took SAKI for SAPPER. *Tray no bong.*
That piece of his, lambasting England's
luxury underclass, was right on target —
SAKI 'as is', Lance-Sergeant BEF.

The moon in its stained ice-clouds; ice-clouds
themselves memorable. How sharply they recall
the years of my late driving, the hoping
not to arrive. IS THIS CANONICAL?
COULD IT BE EPOCH-MAKING? Slow down here;
turn at the volta. Unstoppable work
schedules can only be envied. I need
blanks for the world-surfing quote research
unquote of your average junk-maestro.
BLÁNK BLANK BLÁNK BLANK. BEÉN THERE
DÓNE THAT. My own titles could well prove
épuisés | by instantly wiped applause.

As pellitory, among other common
signatories of the wall, stands to old faith –
step back a step, even if expected –
the fieldstone, intricately veined and seamed;
moss, lichen, dobbed with white crut of birds;
Credo (car radio) | even as I muse
through tactics, passive aggressions, wound-up
laughter from the claques. HAS BEEN | EDITED.
NOT CLEARED FOR PUBLICATION. Don't bleep shop.
Accept contingencies. Honour
the *duende*. Revoke a late
vocation to silence. THÁT'S ALL RÍGHT THEN.

Not to forget Colonel Fajuyi, dead
before I arrived (having lost out to Customs).
Thát means I was robbed; a sweat-pulped cache
of small ten-shilling notes (Nigerian). He
had wórse thíngs to contend with. I don't doubt
his courage, his slow dying — smell my fear! —
protracted hide and seek to the bushed kill. Faithful's
death was as foul but he | went like Elijah.
Remaindered UN helmets, weapons, fatigues,
show up here, neo-tribal. Where did you
ditch the platoon? What have they done with Major
Nzeogwu's eyes?

Old men to their own battles. It may be
troublesome to restart these. On advisement
I make ACTION THIS DAY. And about time.
Carry this through in some order, armatured
at the salute. Even if it kills me.
Empty your pockets for the cage. Re-jig
HM's ageing right profile on sterling
zinc of the realm. Can I say that and not
seem attracted by censure? *Vieillard,*
go to the door. The threshold-angels
will soon come calling. Those with the gifts
have long since been and gone. You were asleep.

INORDINATE | wording of Common Prayer |
find here dilated. Outrage is ripped loose
from the vast scope and body of SORROW,
our hulks moving in convoy. Destroyers —
one has heard of — self-destroyed — boomerangs
from tin fish. Enemas *de rigueur*: no
mud in the proctologist's third eye; no glycol
jellying hís windshield. Nów he expatiates.
POSTERITY | how daring! Waste of effort?
You may conclude so. I do not
so understand it. Yoú may
write this off | but it shall not be read so.

Strange working of the body; how it knows
its ówn tíme. Thát after all | and more —
seventy years near enough — the resin-knurled
damson tree, crookt at black gable-end,
stands in the sight of him departing. LÓRD |
THOÚ HAST BEEN OUR DWELLING PLÁCE — FROM ÓNE
GENERÁTION | TO ANÓTHER (*lento*). So barely
out of step | bow and return. Charles Ives's
Ninetieth Psalm, found late, as grief's thánksgiving;
as full tide with ebb tide, the one in the other,
slow-settling bell arpeggios. Time, here renewed
ás tíme, hów it páces and salútes ús | in its wáys.

53

Fine figure of a man, say it. Try
thís for size. Say it [|] why are we waiting?
Get stuck in. Hurdy-gurdy the starter
handle to make backfire. Call monthlies
double-strength stale *fleurs du mal*. Too close
for comfort [|] say it, *Herr Präsident*, weep
lubricant and brimstone, wipe yo' smile.
COMPETITIVE DEVALUATION — a great find
wasted on pleasantries of intermission.
Say it: licence to silence: say it: me
Tarzan, you [|] diva of multiple choice,
rode proud on oúr arousal-cárrousel.

54

Take it, the plenary immanence, to be
eternal: this passing hence of summer:
and you as being [|] wholly the obscure
origin, the clairvoyance, the giving. *Mein
Ariel, hast du, der Luft, nur ist…?* And by
these words [|] the gifted and recovered
cycles of the unstable, sins not counted.
Contemplation as love's estate, wild aster,
with goldenrod, with the still untorn
awnings of sumac. Consider how thís swáys
argument across the line [|] if
it ís argument. OH I BELIEVE YOU.

55

As many as the days that were | of SODOM.
If thís is to be exorcism. Ís it?
You turn me on. Hoick out another clue.
THE LENGTH OF THE THING. Let them imagine
some signal blessing sent but not received,
saying: Í am in the pink. Wish you were here.
In Abraham's tent and bosom. DID YOU EVER...?
I saíd I believe you ÁND here I háve you.
Among the ellipses | trail-marks cut in salt.
Tristis lupus | I cannot now construe
other than as impeachment. Watch my lips.
Thís is more end-stopped than usual. WHY?

56

Flanders poppy no trial variant. Does
my bad breath offend you? Pick a name
of the unknown YPRES MASTER | as alias.
Abandoned MARK IV tanks, rostered by sex,
Marlbrough s'en va-t-en... frozen mud wrestlers
entertaining the Jocks. Arrest yourself:
for grief of no known cause, excuse me.
A superflux among bit players | which
happens to be the best part: unnatural
wear and tear but finished by Christmas.
Beef of Old England's off. You can eat cake.
YEOMANRY HORSEPLAY FAILS AS LIGHT RELIEF.

57

Shów you something. Shakespeare's elliptical
late syntax renders clear the occlusions,
cálls us to account. For what is abundance
understand redemption. Whó – where – are our
clowns | WET 'N' DRY: will the photographs
reveal all? Só hate to be caught in mid-
gesture, you knów thát, noble CARITAS,
proud AMOR – pledge your uncommon thoughts.
See all as miracle, a natural graft,
as mistletoe ravelling the winter boughs
with nests that shine. And some recensions
better than thát I should hope.

58

Better | than that I should hópe, assign me
to bond with some other fatedness
coveted as free will. I can read
dry-eyed – C. Brontë cleared it with a word –
Olney's own castaway *en famille*. Manic
depressive, wrote about hares. PERFORCE
hís word. Better than that I should hope: my
word is my bond, my surety, my entail.
Twelve press-ups at a time; such heaviness
increased like due allowance. *Entre-nous*
the mad are predators. Forgive me. Cry CHILD
OVERBOARD – the self-righting hull shears on.

Everyone a self-trafficker. I asked
for stone and so received a toad. Alongside |
low-slung jets blizzard the surface-water,
jockey from gate to air-gate: next | the sea-gate
tilts out its lights. Blackness is to be
distinguished from blankness. The Laureates
process blank-faced for you to name them.
Did I sáy another trip ruined by bursts
of atrocious static, England My Country?
Mine, I say, *mine*: damn Skinflint's last onion.
And nów whose England áre you | but then whích
England wére you? Were you ever! NOW THEN!

I think now I shall get throúgh. Even
a bit of a breather. Nothing heavy.
No heavy come-on. Ón thy way, Friend.
Up the Hill | Difficulty. Hów do I find thee?
That's a good name — APOLLYON. Too many
stúck for a treatise maybe | but só whát,
Sister Perversity, ANON on his knees,
sinuses choked with shit. Is there anyone
nót a promoter of simple gifts? Keep
wíth it, PILGRIM | nó more nine days' wonder,
Cambridge, full of thy learning. Flash:
Bucer signs for England — *De Regno Christi*.

Open to every season, the knówn ¦ boúntiful
or as bare for our good. The frosted mantle
over the shot-tower – spectacular –
vivifies cold; once and for all
resumes its corolla, crowns the instant:
I mean the sun's befogged radiance,
our violent infirmities, our dead.
It is not Ceres' living child I see
broken asprawl inside the wind-tunnel,
from limo to limbo in a soundbite,
fuck-up as obligation. ENGLAND AWAKE.
You fell for Aladdin's Uncle – one of thóse.

Witness the untutored, unchastened heart
labouring with its bereavements – thát's
occupied – of time, service; of reward.
Look at the face! But daughters do forgive
fathers – PORTRAIT OF DINORA – unrivalled
even as shadows. The woman. The man.
Grace before arbitration. Is it
the artist only who gets burnt, unalloyed
unallured TETRAGRAMMATON? You
see, I have this blurred vision of Bomberg,
old, dying, *peon* on donkey, lop-
sided, terrible.

Court of Auditors: applause from far back.
Would I have spoken so freely if not
under constraint? EITHER WAY THEY GET YOU.
Providence cited as creditor, who
would credit providence without payment?
Once or twice cheap entr'acte music moves
towards the sublime. Ageing, I am happy.
What price nów forgiveness and likelihood?
Togetherness after sixteen years? You're on.
There ís a final tableau of discovery
and rehabilitation. Not everything
is as we want it.

In for the long haul. Course correction. Go
automatic until relief strikes you: spitted
up to – and beyond – the caecum. No sign there
of most-favoured malignancy. Meanwhile
the sitar's humming-bird finger-blur –
free ín-house video, dizzying
play and replay: life's adjacent realm
with full and frank exchange of love-bites –
how coarse we are, I had forgotten. *Puir
auld sod*. Lift-off but no window. Leibniz's
monad is one thing. Óne thing or another –
we are altogether sómething else agaín.

65

Fragments of short score: inspirational I
find them. Visionary insights also
as they are called. Clouds of dark discernment
part wrath, part thankfulness, the full spectrum
rekindling; the rainbow still to be
fully wrought. Dón't say [|] yoú have forgotten.
I HAVE FORGOTTEN MORE THAN YOU KNOW.
It is not nature but nurture [|] brings
redemption to mind. *Mein Ariel,*
hast du, der Luft, nur ist…? So name your own
sentence. Any sentence. You can have
life if you want it [|] appeal to music.

66

I feel myself the secret keeper of your
engorged smile — this is still my delusion —
Dolores — the sign-language, *bouts-rimés,*
each turn immaculate, drawn, held, on a tight breath,
nothing spoken [|] the crouch and spatter, each
deferring to the mirror. Never a hair
fetishist I am almost ashamed
to confess; have always envied Füssli's
auto-erotic pencil, self-mastery of abasement.
Nothing between lust and friendship [|] one gibed,
though not of Füssli. RE-ENACT THE URINE
CEREMONY: OBSCENITY'S ETIQUETTE.

67

Can't do dialogue even when the dramaturge
purposes confrontation. Snatched asides
pass for exchange. I have composed
clinching *mots de l'escalier* in mid-flight.
The public claims | these besieged privities |
like, when to act entitled by a laugh;
like, kick yourself for courage, doubling up
as your dead stand-in; like, to go under
only to be | insensately revived.
Dolores — LILITH, I shoúld have said —
nothing we did was real. I ask
your pardon. Check my prosthetic tears.

68

Justice: not in order. Valetudinarian
ex-captives to chew dirt. See them sequestered
in alien unforgetting, a lost tribe
whose rites are grief and indignation,
whose speech is primitive, uncomprehending;
incomprehensible, though with a few
loan-words | scavenged from Burmese dialects.
The dead can be struck eloquent. These
dying, cannot — shabbily unsorrowed —
unless you call thís eloquence. GO ON:
Justice | transparent bale-fire of vanities:
massive, shimmering | through incoherence.

Collegiality [|] their grand rule
of unreason, service-formalities
in common disservice. Whát was I thinking –
Bergmanesque tragic farce? I have come
so far [|] anarchy must be in it:
flames ransacking the last scene, as by right
of origin and survival; sheer possession,
threatening the silver [|] and private bride.
No final retribution – háve I saíd that,
and if so, why? Some innocent couple
sleeps through it. Say this was my idea. THÍS
WAS MY IDEA.

As the train curved into Groton [|] I woke
and looked oút for you – whoever you are
or máy be – sadly, without desire (poor
mawkish adverb; either milk it or clip it.
Is that machine turned on?) The State is held
to the character of its citizens. Surrogate
is what Í am. They can have my views
on all such matters: the fabrication
of natural light, the poison-runnels
greening with slick. If not hierarchy
then general dynamics. As the train
curved into Groton I looked oút for you.

I trust that she is now done with the body
search, close interrogation, the finger-
printing, the restless limbo of the *Quais*,
the depilatory | and ritual bath,
the ultimate in cosmetics:
that, for the last time, she has wakened
to cameras, lust, vindictive protocol,
the snarl-ups in the lobby of false friends,
the go-betweens and other betrayers
to public knowledge. I cannot think how
else to commit, commend, her: a botched business,
out of our hands, reduced to the Sublime.

Parrot Prophet X — ad lib PRETTY
BLOODY PRETTY BLOODY. Those bloody Scots
basted in contumacy: new Bannockburn,
old dereliction. Sullen Welsh pride,
the carp half-glimpsed, a glow and shadow
deep amid water-smoke, potent, unheld....
Our Irish trespass, not to be thought of....
Whát phoenix, Coventry — out of whóse fire,
heartless Brummagem, Worcester, grace-abandoned,
self-estranged Althorp, grief's interest,
Handelian measures, freedom hardly won,
forsaken in the act? MAKE RESERVATIONS.

73

A set of courtly clogging dances | I
fancy him | up and doing: kick and shuffle
for solemn cod mugshots, self-artificious
plebeian things of hard edges, effortless
and practised dumb-show. Hís gifts given us
almost in passing – this is not a problem –
as the dance-master floor-chalks original
steps of memory. It is BEHEMOTH
which, among all his works, most flexes
violence under restraint: this being
created neither tó music, nor
fróm music, nór, altogether, fór silence.

74

Bucer's England – *De Regno Christi* – even then
it was not on, not really. The more
you require it, the more it slips from focus,
skews in the frame, the true
commonweal out of true. Bucer knew this,
no-one exempted | nothing of fraudulent
greatness, even so. And Í say: accept
no substitute; but the body's natural
immunity to reason | you máy suffer;
at best by proxy. End of scholastic
disputation. Now the theatricals:
enter SCATOLOGY, *dancing, with* DESIRE.

75

From yoúr vantage, with your latitude,
it may be possible to gaze across –
there's a taped commentary. Call the place
ETRURIA | and watch me signal you,
rehearsed, miming in character, as one
taught to bear up | but nó goód at it.
The bearings must be out, though. Look, we've slipped
two generations, perhaps three; a scene,
noble, sorrowful, in recognition:
stable- or smithy-yard, rough-surfaced
with dirt and clinker-rammel, stomped
by snurring drayhorses.

76

O CLEVER Memory, to take my name
for acts indifferent and true to type.
How formally this begins. There are accidents
you can see coming, whose actual
speed of occurrence is in slow motion.
This is not one. *Ben trovato*, jaws clamp
shut on floating perception and hang there:
now gaffed and despatched. PISCATOR
the ever watchful, curd-faced LADY LUCK.
Just so | I worked the celebrated
elaborate Italian locks, the self-barbed
open-to-shut *concetti* of blind eyes.

77

Revive the antimasque of baroque
methane: time and death — thát rot, a fake
Shakespearean girning, a mouth's pained O,
the soul exhaled | as a perfect smoke-ring,
clownish efforts made to bind the corpse-jaw,
skeletal geezers like kids again with bad
joke-book toothache, Dr Donne's top-knot shroud,
coroneted bag-pudding (*show-off!*). Face
the all but final degradation — FAMED
PILLAR OF THE CHURCH A STIFF — reorder
the Jacobean Sermon, re-set Burton's
Anatomy, endorse the Resurrection.

78

That's great they say | nów I have come thís far.
But still, my brothers and sisters, baroque
ís beautiful. You also have beauty.
Why could I not have foreseen this: we
were meant for each other. Consensual
the gifts of sex, of oratory, in both
unequalled. Ogled by reborn commerce,
nó, I will nót speak straightly | but abide
my chainhood on the block. Ás I can show you:
the bronze equestrian Union trumpeter,
coated with a green patina of swamps,
up from the Wilderness: less strange now than wé are.

Sleep as and when you can. Write this.
We are almost there. *Mein Ariel, hast du,*
der Luft, nur ist…? Captive ⎮ regain
immortality's incarnate lease. Endure
vigil's identity with entrapment.
There are worse obsessions. YOU HAVE MY LEAVE,
GO NOW ⎮ free spirit shaped by captivity,
forsaken in the telling, so to speak,
the end of contemplation: overnight
the first frail ice ⎮ edging across the pond,
self-making otherness by recognition —
even as I describe it.

Ice — *augenblick* — four chordal horns — baritone
invocation of mute powers. The grammar
of the centurion, formed to obedience,
pitched in disorder, unfocused zealotry. THIS
MÁY BE INSUBSTANTIAL. RESUBMIT.
The nadir of your triumph ⎮ to do duty
in place of outright failure, erosions,
worn synapses. Even today the light
is beautiful — you can hardly avoid
seeing thát: shadows — reflections — on reeds
and grasses ⎮ deepening visibility:
the mind's invisible cold conflagration.

81

Again: the saltmarsh in winter. By dawn
drain-mouths grow yellow beards. Old man's duty,
vigilance so engrained, shabby observance,
dirty habit, wavelets chinning the shore-line.
Rich in decrepit analogues ⎮ he sees:
archipelagos, collops of sewage,
wormed ribs jutting through rime. Sun-glanced,
it is striking, vacant, a far consequence,
immaterial reflection beautifully
primed, the decommissioned lighthouse
no longer geared to darkness with clock-shifts
of steady alignment.

82

Plutarchan parallels to special order.
End of a calendar year. The double
lives of lost veterans haunt me. How much
further does this take them? I should guess
nowhere by yoú, openers of the new age,
winners all ways, fawning with sharp elbows,
teeth, to make *lebensraum*, pledging dead loves
to the brokers of Pity, pitiless
resurrection men. O bad luck, Anna,
Boris; bad luck, Dmitri, Laika: you missed us.
Next year same time, same place. Let's all retrench,
get together for sháred únrecognition.

83

Of an age to lapse or revert, bring back
Künstlerschuld, regrettable souvenirs.
Long undetected or overlooked, false
claims of veteran status finally
hauled to account. Even so | childish
anger at the injustice of it. *Jedermann*,
call me *Jedermann*, for the seductive
pleasure of strange mouthings. Say *den Haag*:
heavy old-gold Rembrandts – Dutch-Jewish –
by chance of bestowal: bankrupts, timely
survivors. Making, breaking | things familiar.
At twenty, ignorance was my judgement.

84

Had none or made none. This may as well
tick over, keeping itself vacant
asking for it, conviction. Not transferrable.
Sit as beggars in justice – pardon
the officialdom. And there you háve me.
WELCOME TO THE PEACE PALACE, banging
carillons en suite. As I observed –
twenty-three, *supra* – the Dutch are heroes
living as they have to. Easier said.
I can't say better. Speak as you find.
Whát do Í find? A good question. OVER
TO YOU, BRER FIRE, SENATOR, MISS WORLD.

85

Ruin smell of cat's urine with a small gin.
Develop the anagram – care to go psychic?
Psych a new age, the same old dizzy spell.
Force-field of breakdown near the edge. Nów
to work ⎸ backwards nót like breaking down.
Seek modem-demo, memos to dawn-broker,
duty-savant. CODEBREAKERS our salvation.
Logos of futures, world-scam, meniscus
brinking, about to break, unbroken. Science
not beyond reason. Ultimate hope. Take,
e.g., Democracy – or try to take it –
as cryptic but convenient acronym.

86

He voids each twelve-line blóck ⎸ a head
solemnly breaking water. Not at thís time
Poseidon, but convulsively mortal,
spouting, eyes bulging, green man. Say again –
care to be psychic and by hów múch.
Is there ever a good time? What's on offer?
NIGHT AND FOG ⎸ named as the losing answer
out of thousands submitted: albeit unjust
to slapdash courage. Not all is ruin
if you can hold a final salvo. Rouse
Hipper, advise floundering Jellicoe, make
signal of requiem, cast wreaths of iron.

If I could once focus – Rimbaud's career,
Nigerian careerists – on a single factor,
self-centre of anomie, I might present
to the examiners in whose shadow I am,
a plainly disordered thesis which they
must receive to reject: indifferent
drummers-up for all markets. BIAFRA RULES.
That long-dead young Igbo master who transferred –
so abruptly – his panache and command-flag
from Latin eclogue, from Ovid's *Amores*,
to POLITICS, ESPIONAGE, AND TRAVEL died
with or without judgement. Style undisputed.

Night and fog it ís then, comrades, *Nacht
und Nebel*: goes always for the throat –
pharynx, jugular. Ónce for áll cósts
of live demonstration waived. A few
dead women late admitted heroes
on generous terms. Sign here with broken
hands patched up for the occasion. Thank you
Odette, Violette, no further questions
commensurate with your knowledge. Stand at ease
against the wall. Unflattering photographs,
almost without exception, cracked and stained.
Darkest at finest hour. Add salt to taste.

Write out a cause: crazed sanity [|] untreated
logomachic sarcoma. Unveiled stuff
of grand malpractice. Parts of the interlocked
post-doctrinal foul-up. Cheers! – Augustine's
fellow, who could fart – with most sweet savour –
angels' song: tones passing as angels' song.
Cross-reference ODOUR OF SANCTITY and run.
I give you ten yards cross-examination,
thwart man without allies (with friends, yes).
Don't overstretch it, asshole. Don't say TIME
WIPES ÁLL THINGS CLEAN. Don't let them hear CUR
DEUS HOMO – thát kind of filthy talk.

Mediation means business, the apostles' jets
muster in strength, their afterburners
glowing post-prandial cigars. Mere duty
so empowered [|] it is líke furlough
with millionaires' playthings, a galaxy
of voices, leaping [|] static. Animus
is what I home on, even as to pitch.
You can say thát again. Or not at all.
Split second's chance allowed, no second chance.
My God, he can pack it in – suddenly
come to his temple, its standing [|] here destroyed.
(Rum place for a cigar, *Herr Präsident…*)

Thís lays it ón ˡ a shade: in the arms
of his claustral love. A pun, then, *arms*? He's thát
sórt of a mind. Another one on *lays*:
láys it ˡ on a sháde – are yoú still wíth me?
Wandering again, blocked words húng around neck
on a noose of twine: his ówn náme included.
Not the usual idyll, dazed ingenuities
filling the vacant days. A well-trained child
yawning at the recital. *Mein Ariel,*
hast du, der Luft, nur ist. . .? Teach patience,
SISTER PERVERSITY; how I desired your
variant dolours. FRÍGID BÍTCH ˡ DOLORES!

Either the thing moves, RAPMASTER, or it
does not. I disclaim spontaneity,
the appearance of which is power. I wíll
mátch you fake pindaric for trite
violence, evil twin. Here I address
fresh auditors: suppose you have gone the full
distance. Take up – ón líne – the true nature
of this achievement. Prove that you have fixed
the manifold. Dismiss the non-appearance
of peculiar mercies. Presume to examine
the brain in its electric cauldron
regarding the Brazen Head.

Pardon is incumbent, RAPMASTER, ór it
is nót. On balance I thínk nót. So
get in line, SNÚFF-MAN — with PRINCE OF FEATHERS —
PRATFALL his oppo — mourning Persephone
lost in September tribute, England's daughter.
Hack violence to yourself | brief miracle
confessions overridden. None of these
gífts us self-knowledge: she is beyond it
and you are nowhere | spielers of abuse.
Slów búrn, slów double-táke. The Northampton
MADONNA AND CHILD. She there? Cán it be
the grief matronal? Í shall return to thát.

Hopefully, RAPMASTER, I can take stock
how best to oút-ráp you. Like Herod
raging in the street-pageants | work the crowd.
Bít short of puff these days. Swíg any óne
elixir to revive the *membrum*. Squeeze
bóth tubes for instant bonding. IT'S HÍS CÁLL.
In the Algarve, places like that, the Brits
are heroes | living as they háve to (*cheers*).
Where áre we? Lourdes? SOME sodding mystery tour.
Whát do you meán | a break? Pisses me off.
Great singer Elton John though. CHRIST
ALMIGHTY — even the buses are kneeling!

95

Politics, RAPMASTER, múst be a part
of oúr conformable mystery, this
twinship of loathing and true commonweal.
As yoú haunt Tudor polity [|] so Í
re-gaze the gaze of Holbein, my drawn face
a breath, a dust, of chalk-bloom; pettish
client between porch and easel. Skelton Laureate
was a right rapper: outdance yoú with your shádes
ány dáy. And is góne. Moriscos, hatchet-men,
yoú would have been [|] and are. *De*
Regno Christi: breeding up good and ill,
breaker of Eurostallions.

96

Tune up an old saw: the name-broker
IS carnifex. Forms of enhanced
interrogation by the book. Footnotes
to explain BIRKENAU, BUCHENWALD, BURNHAM
BEECHES, DUMBARTON OAKS, HOLLYWOOD.
Masters of arts toiling as they are bent
to Saturn's justice in praetorian bunkers,
pourrying tortured figures from foundry sand
with suspect blood and their own fecal matter.
As many days as are the days of Sodom:
count áll one hundred and twenty [|] then shriek
I'M COMING.

In re: radical powerlessness of God
to be reconceived. Not for millennial
doom-mood, nihilism's palindrome,
but for what it ís and we áre: no use
against backed-up inertia, ignorance,
proclivity. What was it líke before
Adam made incest with the red earth
his matrix? Their ruination, litter,
our sacred sites for depravity, cells
of Moloch, Baal's palaces: the díscharge
of violence filling the screen – projectile
vomiting en masse.

TAKE TWO: the Northampton MADONNA AND CHILD:
an offering up of deep surfaces; chalk
sleepers from the underground [|] risen to this.
(Moore also became a figure.) Her bulk
and posture, load-bearing rt hip-bone,
inward, understood, projected, wrought.
The chíld's fáce, though, prím, sweetened, incúrious.
Absent here even the unfocused selving
close to vacuity – Stanley Spencer's fixation –
crazed-neighbourly [|] which ís a truth of England
alongside manifest others,
an energy altogether [|] of our kínd.

Hów many móre times? Customs not customs!
Fajuyi was dead by then, though Major Nzeogwu
still had his eyes. Can't you read English? What
do I meán by praise-songs? I could weep.
Thís is a praise-song. These are songs of praise.
Shall I hyphenate-fór-you? Syntax
is a dead language, your incoherence
the volatility of a dead age —
vintage Brook Farm, adulterate founders' bin;
and yoú the *faex Rómuli* | the dregs.
AUTHENTIC SELF a stinker; pass it on,
nasum in ano | the contagious circles.

Onto these near-Stygian sets | the PEOPLE
enters and is discovered: courtesy
Balzac, courtesy Honoré Daumier. Additional
acknowledgements to Balzac, apologies
to Daumier. Could keep this úp all night
rigid with *joie de vivre*. The mountebank
is a poor honest fellow with a drum
and a kitchen chair, a coral-boned
tumbler for a child. The guignol
carries more weight and is, I suspect,
the better artist: fixing on these faces
torpor, avidity — master of light and shade.

Virtue is all in timing; it cán be put
down to instinctive balance: the group leans
into the camera, the unstable darkness.
Let us interpret their eyes, their uncondoned
self-recognition. Look — to be lóst's as good
as being tethered: Oates míght have been found
dead on all fours behínd the tent. But they
sat measuring posthumous averages
of bitter legend. The Great War did not
occur to them. In time | Shackleton cáme
clóse to missing it and was frozen out:
far off the glacier floated | a white feather.

A pale full sun, draining its winter light,
illuminates the bracken and the bracken-coloured
leaves of stubborn oak. Intermittently
the wínd spoórs | over sált ínlets
and the whiteish grass between the zones,
apprehension's covenant. Could this
perhaps end here: a *Paradiso*
not accounted for — unaccountable —
eternally in prospect, memory's blank
heliograph picketing the lost estate?
ÁND | ís this vision enough | unnamed, unknown
bird of immediate flight, of estuaries?

BY AND LARGE: after the renowned, retired,
circus troupe of that name. Cross-
dressing in mid-twist, salvation in mid-fall.
No better choice. Go for baroque. Cán you
máke it? Questions, questions. Show me a mark
of interrogation, I'll show yoú my
exclamation points. Fly me! LOST THE PEACE
BY SUPERHUMAN SKIVING: true or false?
Three out of ten: brave cockney rhyming
slang on an epic scale! Across the board
the Brits are heroes: twenty-four-hour
convenience machismo — IN YOUR FACE!

V. poór linguist, *nota bene*: loved
Latin, German, for love of the uncanny —
unheimlich. What's weird in Latin? Inuit
not too secure (OFFICIAL). Stubborn
metaphysics calls for German above all,
über alles. Where do I gó, *Leiermann*?
Where cán I go? Soul-brother, show a light!
EQUITY, ELIGIBILITY, CULPABILITY,
heard through a cloud — acoustic din — the rage;
that THEATRE OF VOICES, nóble | íf nót
ridiculous. Forsaken in the telling —
pelagic diasporas [LEAVE UNFINISHED]

Absolutely untouched by the contingent –
ás he believes he ís – master
academician of rotor-wisdom,
indispensable, self-made, *thaumaturge*,
until dispensed with | disposed of. THÁT RÍGHT?
What is the present standing of injustice
among those who know? Would we – without Churchill –
have concluded a Vichy peace? That's
hard to say. Daventry and Droitwich
are still transmitting – cries of disbelief,
recognizance | evasions that return
with a comet's faithfulness of assignation.

DE MORTUIS – bitterness of those journeys:
the rail-ice thawed by acetylene
and coke braziers; chipped-free semaphore
arms tílting to right of way. *Arbeit,*
heraús, were nót words Í knew in those
deep years of the dead: the eight-coupled
coal engines, shaken viaducts, compounded
smoke of manufacture and destruction.
If you can still remember, put me down
as terror-stricken, unteachable.
Or hold me to my first promise. *Sadly*
I máy show up in time for yr lást laúgh.

Look on the bright side. WHÁDDYA — WHÁDDYA —
call thís — script or prescription? Cite your own
stiff going-price. Dysfunctional [|] THIS
ALSO IS THOU, NEITHER IS THÍS THOÚ.
Act through a few poor mime faces; pose late
reflexion. As not unreflecting try
posterity. Become vindictive in self-
vindication? Fall then [|] victor among
the secondary infections. Claimed as latest
pastmaster of the grand infarctions —
caught in mid-stride — savaged beyond speech —
(Pray for us sinners) — YOU THÉRE [|] LÁDY?

Not lóve even, aírhead; some *tendresse*
of creatures, young at age. Whát do you knów!
It's better ínside but don't mind clothes.
Share — not nóthing [|] but nót múch: THE POLISH
RIDER is wonderful. When was he
ever in Poland? Even these late
colloquies are fictions. No more games [|]
I can imagine. Responsible
or not, I will hóld you as if — for once —
I would be held ín you. Who is thís?
Come here [|] nearer the light. Are yoú
the Shunammite woman?

Oh, yoú again, DOLORES! I hate shows
of past disaffection; hate-comedies
knocking perverse sainthood. Did the socks
not rot on those feet: for ús beggars?
Thorough-bloodied his potsherds. But new
era, new hero. Am I in error here?
Waked Erin, too – that ís, herself | the grave
setting of comedy. Stout-hearted filmscript
charms loot from Lotto. *Bodhrans* pitch me wild
with dancing excitement. Confirm that? I
sháll | in closed-círcuit confession. ÁND práy
for John Reedy | otherwise Seán Ó Riada.

ÁM discomfited | nót nów being able
to take as fact even my own dying –
the apprehension or prospect thereof. My
faux-legalisms | are to be vouched for,
even if unwitnessed, ás are many things
I could indicate but not show. Whát I see
here | are unfixable fell-gusts | ratching
the cranky chimney-cowls; their smókes blówn
hard dówn or túgged rágged; shade and shine
the chapel wind-vane's blistery fake gold.
I imagine | yoú see this also: súch
is the flare through memory of desire.

111

Míd-stride (*encore!*) sáy I eject from the planet –
if only in spirit – though without notice,
though fully housebroken, drop a dead
weight, shocking, malodorous (draw *pudor*
óver it | let it lie) say: I know myself
in sóme form beholden to grand Orion
long contemplated for yoúr sake | way out
as you cán be; to Andromeda in full
rig, exactly as GURNEY last saw her,
Cassiopeia, her constancy; to the small
unnamed constellation I get to name
Constellation Kreisau.

112

Eight-block coda to the CITY OF GOD –
don't tempt me, Tempter, demon overreacher,
or | nót in my own voice. It was agreed
my topos is SODOM, grandiose
unoriginal. I woúld be myself
stuck in some other *bolge* yet scarcely
recall what it wás I promised, or even
what promise ís | damned liar that I am:
trying on broken accents, reading Dante
as if for the first time – this ís the first
time, better admit it. If back on standard
self-therapy | só much the worse.

113

What is a *vitrine* — how does it connect
with the world of ANSELM KIEFER? This
is what we have cóme to: ash and shivered
glass. Memorialized dead-centres without
focus. Atrocious glamour ⏐ grime-plastered,
corrosive, corroded; road salts, metals.
Single abrupt frame of violent
disassembly: identical frame pulled
back into being. In the obscure
soteriologies of these things, the lines
created are destructive and vital.
Auction. Autopsy. Scrap-avatar.

114

When all else fails CORINTHIANS will be read
by a man in too-tight shoes. No matter. You
shall not degrade or debauch the word LOVE
beyond redemption. As she redeems it.
Six times this trip I have brought round my wreath
to the vulgar gates. Let Thames take over,
not grandiosely, our plebeian grief.
Evangelical high prelates caught
spitting out plum stones [EDIT TAPE]. Guardsmen
make heroic bearers: even their wry-necks
crick in alignment. Comedienne to act
SORRY for hostile nation. CURTAINS. CREDITS.

115

Where CODA to the CITY OF GOD? Restore
whát decrepit organ? Whó has a mind
to improvise? You say it is áll
improvisation — *dú, mein Ariel.*
Shove off, there's a love. Under half-dead
wisteria, crudely cut back, the stone
lintel, newly snail-cobbled, glitters
with their mucilage. Not bad as an aubade;
not quite the final gasp. Extrapolate
LAST POST into reveille. Re evil —
relive, revile, revalue [|] self-
revelation. EASY NOW, SOUL-BROTHER!

116

Hów could you have lived throúgh him [|] so long?
Don't take it for an accusation — you
write as if sleep-walking. I never
walk in my sleep. I fall off chairs. But —
yes — it's a lengthy haul to the diploma.
Self-correction without tears: see me reverse
tango this juggernaut onto the road.
TEN DEGREES BACKWARD, Isaiah says.
Ezekiel's the better mechanic but less —
you know — beautiful! Áll eighteen
wheels engaging the hardtop and no
body-damage to speak of. RIDE IT, PREACHER!

No nearer Jerusalem. Self-justifying
hatred │ taken for all its worth. Worth whát?
Júst as únjust. I know the game,
for and against. Poetics of self-rule.
Why nót twist Luther │ practised self-parodist?
Justified self-accusation at list price.
CAPITALS │ STAGE DIRECTIONS AND OTHER
FORMS OF SUBPOENA. *Italics* │ words
with which Í – *sometimes* – surprise *myself*.
Unapproachable City of God. *Lost
estate* (WESLEY?) │ though if the towers stand │ wróng
way úp │ it's probably *not* a mirage.

Inconstant even in this the dead
heart of the matter: laughter │ no joy.
Thin veil of libel úp for bids. You áre
wantonly obscure, *man sagt.* ACCESSIBLE
traded as DEMOCRATIC, he answers
as he answers móst things these days │ easily.
Except in thís one craft he shows himself
open to a fault, shaken by others' weeping;
duty's memorialist │ for the known-unknown
servants of Empire – for such unburied:
the spirit's gift upheld, impenetrable,
the bone-cage speared by lilies of the veldt.

119

Shambles of peripeteia to discover
history íf not to make it. Loud laughter
track ⎹ poór compensation for the bád shów.
This needs working on but then who needs it?
AMICUS, his own worst enemy? Make a good
ending, as they used to say. So gíve me
yoúr prescription for the good life and I
will teár throúgh it. Dissever sensual
from sensuous, licence from freedom; choose
between real status and real authority.
Clever móve thát — Catullus's sure-
foóted imitation ⎹ of the Límper.

120

English Limper ⎹ after the English Sapphic. Thís
hás to be seen. But whát a way to go.
Given a free mínd Í would present Daumier's
effigies as supreme honours: goúged,
wrenched, and sagging clay; self-made
corruption ravaged ⎹ inexhaustible,
FUROR'S own purity. *English,* you clówn —
líke at the ALDWYCH. So whát cognómen
will become me at last? O TIME-LIFE, dó
try to be reasonable; you háve the power.
At least pass me the oxygen. Too late.
AMOR. MAN IN A COMA, MA'AM. NEMO. AMEN.

About the Author

GEOFFREY HILL was born in Bromsgrove, Worcester-
shire, in 1932. A graduate of Keble College, Oxford, he
taught for many years at the University of Leeds, then
lectured at Cambridge as a Fellow of Emmanuel Col-
lege. He is the author of seven previous books of poetry
and of *New and Collected Poems, 1952–1982*. His stage version
of *Brand*, a dramatic poem by Ibsen, was commissioned
by the National Theatre, London, and performed there
in 1978. His critical writings have been published in two
volumes, *The Lords of Limit* and *The Enemy's Country*, the lat-
ter based on his Clark Lectures delivered at Cambridge
in 1986. Since 1988 he has been a member of The Univer-
sity Professors at Boston University and is co-founder
and co-director of the university's Editorial Institute.

*   *

*